D0773626

# I SPY
## UP IN THE SKY

# THE CLOUDS

BY
TAMRA ORR

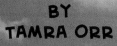

**Mitchell Lane**
PUBLISHERS
P.O. Box 196
Hockessin, Delaware 19707
Visit us on the web: www.mitchelllane.com
Comments? email us:
mitchelllane@mitchelllane.com

**The Clouds**
The Moon
The Stars
The Sun

Printing    1        2        3        4        5        6        7        8        9

**ABOUT THE AUTHOR:** Award-winning children's book author Tamra Orr lives with her family in the Pacific Northwest. Cloud watching is one of her favorite pastimes.

**Library of Congress Cataloging-in-Publication Data**
Orr, Tamra.
 I spy up in the sky the clouds / by Tamra Orr.
     p. cm. — (Randy's corner: I spy in the sky)
 Includes bibliographical references and index.
 ISBN 978-1-58415-974-2 (library bound)
 1. Clouds—Juvenile literature.  I. Title.
 QC921.35.O77 2011
 551.57'6--dc22
                                                                                      2011000727

eBook ISBN: 9781612281445

                                                                                      PLB

# Art in the Sky

Up high in the air,
Scattered across blue skies,
Clouds of all kinds keep
Changing shape and size.

Each one looks different—
Some are high, some low.
Some blow away quickly.
Others drift so slow.

# How Are Clouds Made?

The waters of the world,
Warmed by the sun,
Rise high as vapor
And clouds they become.

They travel the skies,
Move with the wind,
Grow heavy and dark,
And rain down again.

# Back to the Ground

RAIN

HAIL

Clouds send down rain,
Plus hail, sleet, or snow,
Which freeze in the sky,
Then cover below.

**SLEET**

**SNOW**

The fancy name given
To each type of cloud
Tells you its shape, size,
And height from the ground.

9

# Cirrus (SEER-us)
## "Curl of hair, high"

Rows of cirrus clouds—
Lacy, delicate, frail—
Sometimes together
Are called a mare's tail.

They often send out
Strands of fine hair.
These streaks change direction
With a gust of fresh air.

Cumulus clouds are
Puffy and tall.
Don't let them fool you—
Bad weather may fall.

# Cumulus (KYOO-myoo-lus)
## "Gathered," "heaped," or "piled up"

When these clouds form,
Hail often pounds down.
Tornado warnings
May be heard through town.

# Stratus (STRAA-tus)
## "Layered"

Stratus cloud layers
Form with the lifting
Of cool morning fog,
Slowly upward drifting.

These flat, gray clouds
Bring drizzle or snow.
They hide the sunshine
And move away slow.

# Cirrocumulus (seer-oh-KYOO-myoo-lus)
"Curl of hair, high" plus "heaps"

These thin, wispy clouds,
Supercool and high,
Carry ice crystals,
Drop snow from the sky.

Endless rows of white puffs
Ripple across the blue.
They quickly grow large
Or blow out of view.

# Cirrostratus (see-roh-STRAA-tus)
"Curl of hair, high" plus "layered"

These layers of curls
Become thick and white—
Ice crystals inside
Reflect the sunlight.

A sudden halo
Is formed overhead,
Warning the people:
Warm day, rain ahead.

# Stratocumulus

(straa-toh-KYOO-myoo-lus)

"Layered heaps"

Heaped, bumpy layers
Are what you will spy
Through airplane windows
As you fly up high.

Like endless white oceans,
Beyond sight they extend,
Glimmering, soft,
No beginning or end.

# Altocumulus
(aal-toh-KYOO-myoo-lus)
"Mid-height" plus "heaps"

These midlevel clouds
Appear white or gray.
In summer they warn:
"Thunderstorm today!"

They form in long rows,
With small water drops;
They bring in cold fronts,
And warm weather stops.

23

# Altostratus (aal-toh-STRAA-tus)
"Mid-height" plus "layered"


These flat middle clouds
Obscure the sky's blue—
An overcast dome,
That light can't seep through.

Behind blue-gray clouds
A fuzzy moon peeps,
And soon rain or snow
Across the land creeps.

# Nimbostratus (nim-boh-STRAA-tus)

*"Rain" plus "layer"*

Nimbostratus clouds
Fill the sky with gray.
They form a thick layer
That is here to stay.

Heavy with raindrops
This cloud, it's agreed,
Tells people below,
Umbrellas they'll need.

# Cumulonimbus

(kyoo-myoo-loh-NIM-bus)

"Heaped up" plus "rain"

Dark billowing clouds
Rise up strong and tall.
They announce stormy weather,
Warning one and all.

These powerful clouds
Create lightning and more.
When they fill the sky,
Severe storms are in store.

# Clouds from Above

From space, the planet
Is peppered with white.
Astronauts report,
"An amazing sight."

From orbit or Earth,
As the clouds drift by,
We see Nature painting
Her art in the sky.

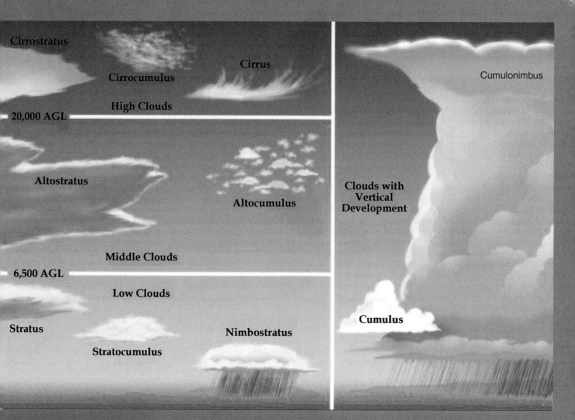

Cirrostratus

Cirrus

Cirrocumulus

High Clouds

Cumulonimbus

20,000 AGL

Altostratus

Altocumulus

Clouds with
Vertical
Development

Middle Clouds

6,500 AGL

Low Clouds

Stratus

Cumulus

Nimbostratus

Stratocumulus

# Words to Know

altitude (AL-tih-tood)—Height above the earth's surface.

alto- (AL-toh)—Middle, or mid (as in mid-height).

cirro- (SEER-roh)—Curl of hair, high.

cumulo- (KYOO-myoo-loh)—Heap.

fog—A layer of stratus clouds near the ground.

halo (HAY-loh)—A round band of color around a light source,
     such as the Sun.

ice crystals (KRIH-stuls)—Tiny pieces of ice that form in clouds.

nimbo- (NIM-boh)—Rain, precipitation.

overcast (OH-ver-kast)—Completely and evenly covering the
     sky.

precipitation (pree-sih-pih-TAY-shun)—Water that falls to
     earth from clouds, in the form of rain, sleet, hail, or snow.

strato- (STRAA-toh)—Layer or blanket.

vapor (VAY-pur)—Fog, mist, steam, or other forms of water gas
     in the air.

# FURTHER READING

## Works Consulted

NASA's Cloud Types. http://asd-www.larc.nasa.gov/SCOOL/tutorial/clouds/cloudtypes_transcript.html

National Geographic's Clouds http://science.nationalgeographic.com/science/earth/earths-atmosphere/clouds-article/

National Weather Service: JetStream—Online School for Weather. http://www.srh.noaa.gov/jetstream/synoptic/clouds.htm

NOAA: Cloud Classification and Characteristics. http://www.crh.noaa.gov/lmk/?n=cloud_classification

Windows to the Universe: National Earth Science Teachers Association. http://www.windows2universe.org/earth/Atmosphere/clouds/altostratus.html

## Books

Graf, Mike. *How Does a Cloud Become a Thunderstorm?* Mankato, Minnesota: Heinemann-Raintree, 2009.

Rockwell, Anne. *Clouds*. New York: Collins, 2008.

Rodgers, Alan. *Sunshine and Clouds*. Mankato, Minnesota: Heinemann Library, 2008.

Taylor, Geraldine. *What Are Clouds Made Of? And Other Questions About the World Around Us*. New York: Cartwheel Books, 2008.

Tomkins, Jasper. *Nimby: An Extraordinary Cloud Who Meets a Remarkable Friend*. Seattle: Green Tiger Press, 2011.

## On the Internet

Clouds at Weather WizKids http://www.weatherwizkids.com/weather-clouds.htm

Cool Clouds for Kids of All Ages http://www.pals.iastate.edu/carlson/main.html

Geography for Kids: Clouds http://www.kidsgeo.com/geography-for-kids/0109-clouds.php

Web Weather for Kids http://eo.ucar.edu/webweather/cloud3.html

# INDEX